From DEATH to DANCE

*One Person's Journey From the Darkness
and Despair of Death to the Lightness
and Joy of Dance*

DR. JANET M. BIESCHKE

BOOKSIDE Press

BookSide Press
877-741-8091
www.booksidepress.com
orders@booksidepress.com

Contents

Foreword

"From Death to Dance: *One Person's Journey from the Darkness and Despair of Death to the Lightness and Joy of Dance*" chronicles the author's transformative path from profound grief to renewed vitality through the art of dance. Central to this metamorphosis is the Fred Astaire Dance Studio, which provided not only expert instruction but also a supportive community that embraced the author during a time of deep sorrow. The studio's nurturing environment and the joy of movement became pivotal in the author's healing process, illustrating the profound impact that dance and compassionate mentorship can have on personal recovery. This inspiring narrative serves as a testament to the resilience of the human spirit and the therapeutic power of dance.

—By Stephen Knight, Vice President & Executive Dance Director, Fred Astaire International.

"From Death to Dance" is a compelling memoir that illustrates the profound healing power of dance. Dr. Janet's journey from deep despair to joy through her experiences at Fred Astaire Dance Studios mirrors the transformative stories of many of our students. Engaging in dance fosters emotional resilience, physical vitality, social connections, and mental clarity. Witnessing such positive changes in our students reaffirms the significant impact of dance on holistic well-being.

—Hayk Arshakian, Wisconsin Area Director
& International Dance Council Member

WHAT OTHERS ARE SAYING

Through your eyes and through your words, I found a renewed sense of inspiration for this beautiful art we call dance.

Your story is deeply touching, having taken me on an emotional ride yet I could still smile at the gifts of revelation you shared.

Your poems are words of wisdom that serve as "life reminders" to never underestimate the power of perseverance. What a blessing dance has been to you and hopefully many others will benefit from your story.

Thank you for sharing.

—Nadia Eftedal, Open British Champion
UK and Open Champion US

The author has written from her own direct experience of using the physical body and movement, in the form of dance to transform grief into passion and move from despair to renewed gusto for living. Her healing process is an inspiration for anyone challenged by profound loss. The physical body is a powerful vehicle through which we can heal and recover through the act of sacred movement. Movement is medicine!

—Elise Cantrell, author teacher, and alternative healer.

"As dress designers who have spent years working with competitive dancers, we see firsthand the transformative power of dance. We watch students step onto the dance floor burdened by life's struggles, only to be lifted by the rhythm, the movement, and the sheer joy of expression. From Death to Dance captures this profound metamorphosis in a way that is both deeply personal and universally inspiring.

This book is a testament to the resilience of the human spirit. The author's journey from loss and despair to healing and renewal through dance is one that will resonate with anyone who has ever sought solace in movement. As someone who outfits dancers for their most important moments—competitions, performances, and milestones—we understand the significance of dance not just as an art form, but as a lifeline.

What struck us most about this story was the raw honesty with which the author shares her pain, as well as the unshakable determination that led her to the dance floor. It is a reminder that dance is more than just technique and artistry; it is therapy, community, and a source of joy that can pull us from the darkest of places.

For those who dance, this book will reaffirm what they already know—that the ballroom is a place of transformation. For those who have yet to discover its magic, From Death to Dance will be a compelling invitation to step onto the floor and find themselves in the music. This is a must-read for dancers, instructors, and anyone who believes in the power of movement to heal."

—Erik Petrosyan & Margarita Taryan
Founders & Designers of Petrosyan Designs

Acknowledgments

This book is dedicated to my daughter Maria. I hope you are dancing in a heaven full of loving spirits.

It is also dedicated to the parents of dancers and the support you give to your children. It takes your time and financial sacrifices, and you may not see the rewards for many, many years. It pleases me greatly to see some of my grandchildren dancing. My heart is happy when any of my family comes to watch me dance. I appreciate your love and support.

I especially want to acknowledge the mothers of Magdalena and Przemyslaw. I see the rewards of your commitment, and I appreciate and thank you.

I am a work in process, or is it a work in progress? I am full of light and full of darkness. I am in the process of picking up pieces and wanting them to be put back together in the ways I remember.

It will never be together as it once was. Therefore, it will be a work of progress towards something better.

I still have hope for the better. Maybe our paths will cross in ways that reflect joys for each of us. Welcome to this process of progress.

Shall we begin? The book without end.

It's been a year since I've finished writing the majority of this book, and you may notice that with some of my references to time. I have been waiting to discover the appropriate ending. I still wait!

Many times when I am seeking guidance or asking God for something, I include a sign of my impatience by wanting it to come now. Like NOW. And obviously that has not happened.

But after a year and realizing that maybe there is no big ending other than the fact I'm still here (I didn't want to be), it's time to just wrap this up. Maybe that is enough proof that I have already danced out of the other side of my hell. At least that's the way Susie E., a fellow life coach, described my journey.

There are now additional questions that seem to be ever present.

The first is what needs to be created. And the second is, who have I come here to be?

As I ponder these questions, I realize that so many people have provided feedback on how they've been inspired by my story. To you, I am grateful for our connection.

So I will share this part of my story in the hope that it provides a connection to your light and your source energy. That's also asking you to find what needs to be created in your life and who you have come here to be. Together, this is a journey that allows us to discover elements created at the moment of our inception—those gifts that may be lying dormant waiting for us to unwrap them and use them. I invite you to come with me on this continuing journey.

As in our dance lessons, repetition leads to clarity. It is how we explore, learn, and eventually create clarity. You will find repetition in this book. I believe that when we retell our stories, we find different ways to explore our words, to see and to learn the possible lessons, and to find clarity. In this process, we learn and grow. I will write of some sad times; however, I will fill the pages with only happy times, laughing and learning times, and joyful experiences of life as I now know it.

This is an interactive book, so I suggest that you grab a pen and consider this book to be your workplace. It is not intended to be a novel that you read from cover to cover. Take your time. You may find it useful to just randomly open it up and see what shows up for you. Mark it up. Highlight words that speak to you. Capture questions and thoughts that cross your mind as you read. You've purchased this book, so make it personal and enjoy your journey.

One change before publishing this book was to give it an underlying theme to allow for a smoother transition between chapters. I've chosen the lighthouse. I often observe people who stand symbolically as this lighthouse for others without even realizing the many ways their light illuminates and connects to others. In living and navigating powerful storms, they offer both support and guidance.

This is powerful because in the end, it is not the absence of the storm, but the presence of the light that guides us forward.

Life / Dance

REFLECTIONS

In looking back, there were times I just went through the motions without knowing where the future would lead. Fortunately, there were always others to stand beside me and to guide me.

When I have no words and so many rapid-fire thoughts and emotions, I sit with a pen in hand and allow the thoughts to swirl until they are ready to drift onto a blank sheet of paper.

I have no particular style of writing other than to capture thoughts and put them into words. My poetry bounces in no form other than sometimes it is worth keeping. In the first grade, we were all given a book of poems that we were to memorize. The only thing I remember is that it was called

The Little Red Book of Poems. I have since filled and trashed a few binders of things that may have fallen into that category.

I entered a poem titled *Open Soul* into the Chicago 2011 IBAM (Irish books, authors, and music) event, and was pleased with a second-place award. It gave me just enough courage to keep dabbling with my words. If I find a copy, I will share it only because it was funny. It was about being a child and preparing for a Saturday confession. We had a Book of Sins that we read so we could recall our sins of the previous week. It seemed insincere to confess a sin, perform the given penance, and then commit the same sin the following week. It didn't seem as though we had many choices. The part of the poetry I recall was, 'Who knew one couldn't commit adultery at the age of ten?'

I have periods of nothingness, and suddenly I awake with ideas, thoughts bouncing in every direction full of quotes and poems. If possible, I stop everything and try to capture these on scraps of paper. I have scraps of paper in my kitchen, bedroom, and vehicle and sometimes left in my pockets. Some of the latter have met a quick demise by going through the washing machine.

Other times, I will grab the phone and use voice-to-text technology as the quickest method of getting these thoughts on paper. Now I'm attempting to organize this collection into something that makes useful sense for you.

Much of what follows is a collection of these thoughts and quotes over this past year. Some are admittedly still too dark to capture—yet.

Have you ever felt that your life was too good, too blessed, that you were too lucky? Even with the crazies of the world, deep down you realized that your family was all doing good, your health was manageable, your career had been overall a success, and you'd reached a point where you were giving back and that you had a whole lot to be thankful for during life?

Having been on a life's high almost forty years ago, I knew that was a risky feeling. It was almost as if acknowledging it was sure to bring about a disaster. The thought was there shortly before my first marriage was shattered and collapsed into divorce. It took much time to learn to trust and rebuild; however, it happened, and the marriage to follow was even better, stronger, more stable, more fun, and full of trust.

For thirty years, life bounced with ups and downs. Work, health, family, finances, age, and loss of parents rolled through as we learned to accept the pendulum shifts. Love was ever-present, life was fun: we knew we were blessed. We completed our advanced directives knowing we were losing friends. After retiring, I had become certified as a hospice volunteer and found the rewards of interviewing hospice patients and others facing death. Richard and I had many discussions about end-of-life issues. We agreed that quick and painless would be a good way to go if given a choice.

We always think we will have more time. We were healthy and seemingly quite active. We traveled, visited more with family, and had time for friends.

Though this book will cover stories of death, its primary focus will be on a story of life, of living, and how dance became an unexpected tool. I intend to fill it with happy pictures. Even when I write about sad things. Especially when I think and write about the sad things.

For the record, I do not dance. In over 70 years, I've never danced. Other than enjoying a few slow dances with Richard while at a wedding or two, I don't really like dancing. I've only watched *Dancing with the Stars* when Green Bay Packers wide receiver Donald Driver participated. It's not my thing and wasn't even on my bucket list.

Actually, I didn't have a bucket list. I had a very blessed life. Until it wasn't.

Because the wonderful life that I talked about changed drastically four years ago when our grandson decided that he would douse himself with a gallon of lighter fluid and lit himself on fire thus beginning a horrific change in our life. Why he did this, I will never know. I will never understand. I no longer ask why as I have come to accept the fact that for whatever reason it was his choice, it was his decision. It was the way that his life would end.

I would like to tell you how it shaped my perspective because I know it has. Unfortunately, I have no way to put those feelings into words. When I think of him, the sadness is profound and I wonder who he would be today. I cannot condemn him for his choice, I do not want to accept it, but none of that matters. The only good thing that came out of that decision of his was that one month before he committed suicide, he did go to the Department of Motor Vehicles and signed his organ donor card. He subsequently was able to give life to five other people, and for this, I am thankful because it is the one thing that seems like a positive outcome from an otherwise negative choice. Suffice it to say his action negatively affected many lives.

I would like to say that amid the waves of loss, I found an unexpected lifeline in the dance studio, but it would be several years before that healing came. It would be nice for all of us if the healing would come immediately after our losses; however, that's not the way it works. Eventually it would be in the rhythm of movement and the embrace of connection where I would begin to rebuild. However, it would take time and many changes before I found the connection of the dance studio.

Within six months, our nation and our world learned the different ways restrictions would come to us via COVID-19 and how much of our world would be shut down. Personally, it stopped me from doing my hospice volunteering. I could no longer go sit with someone who is actively dying to be with them in their final moments. In fact, everything about my volunteering quickly came to an end because I could not enter a nursing home, hospital, or someone else's home.

It was within this early stage of Covid-19 that my husband had a massive heart attack, and though he was kept on life support for a few days, it was only long enough for the medical people to determine there really was no life remaining. The term they used was brain dead. He was switched to comfort care, which means when his body decided to completely shut down, he would be gone.

Without all of the details of that, it came at a time when there was already loneliness in the world. There was already isolation in our lives. What it did was prevent us from having that end-of-life closure. There wasn't a funeral allowed during those times. The gatherings in churches were shut down. People did not come to our home to express sympathies, to offer condolences, to share stories, or to remind me of the good times in his life. It was a time of very quiet emptiness.

Even in emptiness, there were paths waiting for me to find and to follow. I will describe the main path that would guide me forward. It was the people along the way who served as my guide, motivation, and inspiration.

If our paths have crossed, I thank you for whatever role you have played in creating this dancing memory collection. If our paths have not yet crossed, I look forward to the time when it happens.

A good perspective for a new dancer is to approach each step with patience, curiosity, and a willingness to learn. Embrace the journey of self-discovery through dance and remember that making mistakes is a natural part of the process. Enjoy the music, the movement, and the connections you make on the dance floor, as they can enrich your life in unexpected ways.

Learning patience in the dance of life is like mastering a graceful waltz. Just as every step takes time to perfect, every moment in life unfolds at its own pace. Embrace the rhythm, enjoy the journey, and trust that with patience, you'll dance through challenges and triumphs alike with elegance and grace.

I've selected five categories to serve as inspiration for different aspects of life and the metaphors we can draw from dance to understand them.

1.
Growth and Learning

There are moments and experiences all through life that allow for our growth and our learning. This is true even though it's not always easy to find these moments during our darkest empty times in life. Yet it is possible to receive unwanted growth through grief. I learned that it was possible to smile on the outside and to trust the people surrounding me. The dance instructors have found the ability to always extrapolate happiness from every experience.

Maybe it was their energy that propelled me through the inside struggles. I have learned that most people carry burdens, and many of us have become masters of pushing down emotions while pushing forward with actions. Smiles and laughter eventually seep into our hearts and souls. The studio was the perfect setting for this. The instructors engage with all the students. Someone captured this moment when Emily was my playful partner in crime.

As the lighthouse will serve as my metaphor here, we will see it doesn't avoid the storm, but it stands firm in the face of it. Likewise, during difficult emotional periods, our growth comes from confronting the storm rather than fleeing from it. Life is guaranteed to bring each of us waves of hardship especially as we grow older. These waves, though powerful, shape the rocky shore over time, just as adversity shapes us. With each wave, we learn something new about ourselves, about the world, and also about our capacity to endure.

When an unexpected death comes and takes our breath away, it leaves us in the midst of what seems like an endless night.

This following story from 2019 reflects how we may feel when our own storms come raging through us. It was a summer night when my adult granddaughter called me as I was preparing to end my day. As a personal rule, I avoid answering phone calls after 10 p.m. Because it was so unusual for me to get a call from her this late at night, I picked up the phone. She was calling to tell me that her older brother had just attempted suicide by dousing himself with a gallon of lighter fluid and then lighting himself on fire.

What a horrific scenario! She proceeded to say that he was currently being transported to the Madison Burn Center by Flight for Life. That was enough information to let you know that this was both a tragic and traumatic experience for everyone who cared about him.

I cannot describe the overwhelming sense of sadness and helplessness that took away so much light from our lives. He was twenty-four years old. Personally, for me, his death would be the first of seven within the next two years. The only beam of light from that first death was that one month earlier, he had made a visit to the Department of Motor Vehicles (DMV) where he changed his driver's license to include the word DONOR. Though it came with little joy, we understood that his subsequent death had given the gifts of life to others. For each of those organ recipients, he and the choices he made provided a beam of light.

When it feels like there's no light left in our world, a tiny beam from someone is all it takes to serve to cut through the darkness. It can show a path forward, however weak that light might be shining. Sometimes it's that tiny bit of light that emerges from within us when life feels most uncertain. This light is what we each carry and share.

Our grandson left a large hole in our hearts at the very same time he served as a beacon of light to at least five other families who would receive the call they so desperately needed and awaited.

The lighthouse serves not only as a guide to ships but also stands as a symbol of perseverance during our darkest times. Each lesson learned, no matter how small, becomes like a brick added to the foundation of our resilience. Each new insight, each new dance step, each physical or emotional change, and every moment of clarity amidst the fog strengthens us, enabling us to shine more brightly.

It seems that our life is intended to be a dance of continuous learning, with each step revealing new wisdom and hopefully more growth.

In the dance of life, we grow by embracing every misstep and stumble as a chance to learn.

In life's dance, every misstep is an opportunity to grow. I am very fortunate to have a patient and an extremely kind instructor who constantly reminds me that even mistakes can lead to new learning. During a recent competition, we were on the dance floor, and I did something unexpected (aka a misstep). Rather than become upset with me, he just smiled and said, "That was an interesting new dance move." I appreciate his teaching style immensely, as his positive responses turn my missteps into lessons.

> In the grand ballroom of existence, we sway,
> To the rhythms of night and the light of day.
> Life's dance, a tapestry of steps and turns,
> Where growth and learning are the fire that burns.
>
> With each new dawn, a chance to pirouette,
> To embrace the wisdom that we haven't met.
> In every misstep, we find our way,
> As we grow and learn in the dance of today.
>
> The choreography of time, ever changing,
> Through joy and pain, we keep rearranging.
> With open hearts, we take our place,
> In the ceaseless dance, the human race.
>
> From the first wobbly steps to the final bow,
> The journey of learning, we fervently vow.
> Life's dance, a poem written with our feet,
> In its intricate steps, our souls find their beat.

So let us dance with courage, without fear,
In the pursuit of knowledge, year by year.
For growth and learning, the heart's true chance,
To waltz through life's beautiful intricate dance.
(shortened)
In life's ballroom, we sway and spin,
Through the night and day, new wisdom begins.

In missed steps, we find our way,
Learning, growing, day by day.
The choreography ever shifts,
Through joy and pain, we find our gifts.

From wobbly steps to a final bow,
Life's a dance, here and now
With open hearts, we take our stance
And waltz through life's intricate dance.

In the stillness after the storm, the lighthouse remains a little weathered but unbroken. A disappointing dance may offer much room for reflection and growth. Similarly, after a period of emotional darkness, we emerge stronger, wiser, and more deeply rooted in who we are.

Growth during these times is not always visible immediately, but like the lighthouse, it is steady, persistent, and ultimately transformative. The darkness doesn't stop the light from shining. In fact, it's in the darkest moments that the light of growth and learning is most needed and most visible.

This is where it becomes personal. I again invite you to use the clarifying questions at the end of each section for reflection and possible growth and learning.

Clarifying Questions to Self:

What challenges me?

What inspires me?

How do I show up as a student in life, in dance, or with others?

Looking back in my life, I've learned so much. Here are a few things that I'm most proud of having accomplished:

I feel good about my ability to learn, and this inspires me to do even more. What is my next goal?

More quotes for reflection:

In the garden of Dance and Life, the seeds of preparation and the care of cultivation bear the sweetest fruit on the stage.

In the dance of life, when climbing tall mountains, remember: one step at a time leads you to the summit of your dreams.

In the dance of life, the desire to learn is a beautiful step, but let's not burden our instructor with the weight of wanting too much too soon.

In the grand ballet of life, the success of the big performances is woven from the graceful steps taken on the ordinary days.

Dance life is a symphony of preparation, but sometimes we get lost in the noise of other distractions.

Dance is the expression of life, and fear is the shadow that dances alongside, but when we move with courage, fear becomes just another step in the rhythm of our journey.

In the intricate dance of life, the best instructors are those who gracefully waltz through their students' traumas, helping them find healing steps and rhythms for health, death, divorce, etc.

In the grand ballroom of life, dance instructors, not trained as therapists, can lead us to the answers we seek. Sometimes, the simplest question, 'Shall we dance?' unveils the most profound solutions.

In the grand dance of life, we end competitions not with a victor's pose but with a glance of acknowledgment. Then, we ask the question, 'What's next?' and gracefully move on to embrace the rhythms and surprises that life brings.

As the new week begins, step onto the dance floor of life with enthusiasm, for it's in the rhythm of each day that opportunities gracefully waltz your way, waiting to be embraced.

In the grand ballet of life, it's often in the graceful pauses of silence that we discover the true guiding steps forward.

Life's dance tests her patience, and after the most challenging steps, she quits—but then returns, enticed by the rhythm of the same irresistible song.

When she says, 'I'll shut up and follow,' it's her way of whispering to God, the universe, 'Guide me with strength, lead me through life's intricate dance, for in surrender, she finds her true direction."

In the dance of life, sometimes we finish a lesson before we've learned all the steps. Embrace the beauty of the unfinished choreography, for it's in the gaps that we find space for growth and transformation.

The answer to not being able to remember a dance step is to learn another new step; for in every misstep, there's an opportunity for a graceful recovery.

Life's dance demands that we take the student's responsibility, preparing ourselves earnestly before inviting the teacher, for only in our readiness do we truly learn the steps to our own unique choreography.

She contemplates how to convey to her dance instructor that he saved her life, though all he did was teach her to dance, unaware of the profound impact of his actions.

Life is a dance, and with every step, we grow and learn. Just as a dancer practices to perfect their art, we must embrace each experience, for it is our ultimate teacher on this ever-evolving dance floor of existence.

Dance is the music of life, and to the many experienced, talented coaches who are the choreographers of our success. Thank you for your willingness to help perfect our techniques!

There will always be at least a few times when life seems to take the wind out of our sails. This happens no matter who we are, how smart, how beautiful, how successful, or who we know. These will be the times we must reach deep to connect to our anchor. It may be our family, our faith, our friends, or complete strangers that God steers onto our path. This connection is our grounding cord.

Over the years we began to appreciate that anchors are always available when life takes us down deeper than we ever imagined possible. The more this occurs, the more we become aware of our personal strengths and our differing levels of resilience. The more we begin to trust this to be true, the more we will appreciate it, and then also understand and believe that we have the ability to adapt to the changes. These anchors provide us with resilience. If we are willing to adapt along the way, our growth and learning become more apparent and will continue to expand.

2.
Resilience and Adaptability

We may search from side to side as we look for those who will be able to guide us. They will be those who provide direction, timing, and encouragement. They also provide us with the ability to take on new directions. They provide support until such time that our confidence allows us to adapt and to become strong enough to notice our resiliency. In the following, it was both Przemyslaw and Arsen guiding this dance.Like a skilled dancer,

resilience allows us to gracefully recover from the stumbles of life. Whether dancing as an amateur or a pro, we all stumble. It happens both on and off the dance floor. It happens in front of others and while we are completely alone. We may laugh through our stumbles; we may be embarrassed, or we may even cry. Know they are there and will continue to show up. If we learn to adapt to them, we may see how they add to our strength. Life's dance will be unpredictable and may change its tempo, but our adaptability keeps us in rhythm.

The lighthouse represents our inner strength: strong, unwavering, and anchored deep beneath the surface. The lighthouse also represents the whole dancing organization: the owners, the leaders and office managers, the teachers, staff, and sometimes our fellow students.

Just as the lighthouse shines its light into the darkness guiding ships safely through the treacherous waters, resilience is the inner light that continues to shine even when everything around may feel overwhelming or empty. It doesn't prevent the storm from raging, but it provides direction—a constant reminder that despite the chaos, there is a way through.

The approaching storm was building force.

When my daughter called from the Milwaukee hospital to tell me she had just been diagnosed with acute myeloid leukemia, I also learned that because of Covid-19 restrictions, I would not be allowed to be with her during her chemo and radiation therapy. I would not be able to put on the masks, gown, and gloves to just be in her room as did complete strangers entering for spiritual purposes or similar to the care givers. Seven weeks from this diagnosis, she would be dead. I was angry!

As we had recently held my husband's services, I was already in an unstable emotional state. I was reeling. Hers would be the third death during this period, and you may understand why my emotions were raging.

Had she been in a different hospital within Milwaukee, they would've allowed her to have one visitor. So, it was the same Covid concerns, same city, same diagnosis, but with a totally different outcome.

She could not be transferred until being released, and she wasn't able to be released. I was so frustrated, angry—and as a mother, overwhelmed with a sense of parental failure. No matter their age, your child is always your child, and when they are in need, you naturally want to go to them. Alone, angry, frustrated, concerned, and so much more. I did not feel any sense of strength or of resilience.

Our grandson Jacob's suicide was a shock to all of us. Richard's death had left me with many questions to answer. Most of them were 'how' questions:

How do I continue to live without him?

How do I maintain different parts of the home or yard?

How do I fix things that he had previously been responsible for handling?

How do I even know what needs to be done and when?

How do I find the parts of me that will somehow make life worth living again?

My daughter's death brought different types of questions, and most of them were 'why':

Why her and not me? This was the main one that repeated over and over and over.

Why hadn't they caught this earlier?

Why do I stay?

Why do I even want to stay?

But my sister's death and the subsequent ones that followed brought numbness. I could no longer feel. I could no longer think. I could no longer rationalize, and I could no longer function properly. I no longer had questions. I didn't care.

I was empty.

I was nothing.

I had mostly stopped thinking.

I guess I would fit the definition of being a zombie.

I was nothing. Absolutely nothing.

Yet here I was.

Why?

This was all during the Covid era. No one came to visit. Social functions had all ceased to exist.

Most places where I may have run into people had closed their doors either from regulation, fear, or health concerns.

I didn't go anywhere, and no one came here. After acquaintances had made the obligatory calls or sent the condolence cards, even those personal connections stopped. I understood. I was living under a huge black cloud, and no one wants to deal with that. What would they say, and what difference would it have made?

I understand that there was nothing positive about having a conversation with me. I also understood that so many people were struggling with the changes. Some had lost jobs; others were concerned that they may soon lose their jobs. Some were experiencing illness, death, and other problems unknown to me.

Yet through all of it, two people remained constant during those first few months. One was Denise, a former colleague who made it a point to check in with me on a regular basis. The other was my brother Patrick. These two were each a godsend! They were my connection to the outside world.

The regular calls from these two continued through that first year and were flickering lights that continued to shine. They connected me to my lighthouse.

No matter how isolated or lost we may feel, like ships at sea, we are drawn back towards the safety of the consistent light of resilience.

It took time as, in this situation of being powerless, there was also an inability to pray to the very God who was supposedly in charge, allowing this disease to take Maria's life. Angry and empty with nowhere to turn, I needed a lighthouse and eventually found that indeed, one was close.

Our instructors are not trained to be psychologists or therapists, yet there are moments when they become something much more—our Lighthouses. In the midst of our personal storms, when the world feels too heavy to carry alone, they offer a safe haven. With nothing more than a quiet understanding and the simple, powerful invitation of 'let's dance,' they guide us through the darkness, reminding us that even in our most vulnerable moments, there is always a way forward.

They serve as the foundation—strong and built to stand relentless winds and waves. Through moments of difficulty, by trusting in our own strength and with their guidance, we are reminded that we too can endure the darkest nights until calmer waters arrive. In the end, it is not the absence of the storm but the presence of the light that defines resilience. I found, in addition to my family, that the dance studios and the people that I encountered while there served as my bright lights.

I realize that during my first year of dancing, I depended too much on the emotional capacity of my instructors. They were considered to be my earth angels. It had been a little more than two years after my husband had died and a little more than a year after my daughter had died when I began dancing. In my own terms, I was still an emotional mess.

A simple touch could trigger emotions that I was unprepared to feel. I'm certain I owe them many boxes of tissues as a certain song would hit me the wrong way and leave me flowing in tears. One of my early instructors, Victor, said I was the only student he knew who could dance the tango while crying. I called these my free face washes, and they lasted through the entirety of my first year of dancing.

One day while in the studio, a young adult daughter of another student came in to bring a cellphone to her mom. Of course, the student wanted to introduce us to her. It hit me like a ton of bricks when I heard the words "Hi, Mom"

I knew that my daughter would never again walk into any part of my life to do even the simplest of things. I couldn't even walk over and be introduced to this young lady. My instructor's sensitivity noticed my reaction, and he handed me a tissue and suggested a break. Sometimes there are no words, just an ability to acknowledge the hurt.

Now, though there may be a certain touch or a song that touches my heart, I can simply look up and appreciate the spirit presence that I feel guiding me in the form of my late husband or daughter. My emotions are better controlled. They are still there, but not with the same turbulent strength or frequency as before.

One of my great granddaughters gave me a gift when she described my daughter's death very succinctly. At the age of three years, she made the statement "Grandma lost her body." I asked her to repeat what she had said. Again, she said, "Grandma lost her body."

In that context, she was correct. My daughter was still here—just not in her body. I had never heard death described so simply or succinctly. I still believe that young children carry messages to us. Being fresh from heaven, they know things we have long since forgotten. At times, I do still feel her presence. If you've lost someone close to you, you may realize how powerful that spirit presence can be and how long it can remain.

Because as the lighthouse stands tall, amidst the shifting, unpredictable sea, so do the constancy and dependability of the dance studio and the instructors.

The lighthouse is built to endure all kinds of weather, whether it's the calm of a clear day or the fury of a storm. In the same way, resilience is the ability to remain steadfast when life throws challenges our way; no matter how rough the seas get or how fierce the winds blow, the lighthouse doesn't falter; it stands its ground, firm in its purpose.

In life's dance, resilience and adaptability are the partners that twirl us through the ever-changing rhythms, helping us find grace even in the most challenging of steps.

Dance often demands physical, mental, and emotional resilience as dancers overcome challenges, push limits, and adjust to different styles, environments, and partners. So adaptability is key, where we must be flexible and willing to make changes.

Because resilience alone is not enough for any of us. The lighthouse, though unmovable at its core, has a light that moves. It's ever turning slowly, sweeping its beam across the waters. This light is its adaptability, adjusting to the needs of the ships that rely upon it. It doesn't claim to have one fixed direction but continuously adjusts, illuminating different parts of the sea.

Many times, the planned dance choreography is changed because I struggle to follow it or because my instructor finds a better technique.

And yet there are other times when I want a change that my instructor will stand firm because he has knowledge that I do not, and he knows what is more effective for my learning. I have learned to trust this.

Likewise, being adaptable means we can adjust our approach to life's challenges without losing sight of our core values or our strength. It's the ability to respond to change, to shift our focus, and to find new ways forward when the path seems to be totally blocked. At times I believe I am guilty of blocking my own path. Maybe that just means I'm being guided into a new direction. I am learning to follow this intuition.

In life's dance, we're taught to be free,
To sway with the winds, like a resilient tree.
In every twist, we learn to survive,
With adaptability, we come alive.

When music shifts and steps grow tough,
Resilience within is more than enough.

Through storms or calm, both day and night,
We dance through all with steadfast might.

With grace, we pivot as obstacles near,
In adversity's face, we conquer fear.
Life's choreography is a shifting art,
Where resilience and adaptability play their part.

So let us dance with hearts held high,
In the ballet of life, we reach the sky.
Resilient and bold, we find our way,
Shining brighter with each day.

I constantly find myself analyzing situations and assessing their value. One recent example occurred at the National Dance Competition in Florida. Attempting to manage my budget, I did not participate. But I did follow my fellow students and their many successes via social media. I watched them dancing.

Honestly, I became aware of my feelings of disappointment, and a touch of jealousy surfaced. At my age, it is highly unlikely that I will ever attain the levels of dancing that my role models possess. I do not have their experience and know that I never will. I accept that.

Simultaneously, I appreciate knowing that we have access to the same dance partner, who is a brilliant teacher and who works miracles on the dance floor. I appreciate knowing such excellence all around me. I am exposed to very high-level dancing with every interaction. This is true in every competition and also true in all activities at the local studio: parties, lessons, and other activities.

We are blessed to have so much experience and expertise in the Fred Astaire Dance Studios. It's now your turn to appreciate some of your strengths.

Clarifying Questions to Self:

What are my strengths that others have noticed in me?

Which do I value the most?

How do my strengths pull me through life's challenges?

I am most resilient when I stop and value 'these' things that have always given me strength in the past:

Whether it's silence, reflection, prayer, music, or time with supportive people, 'these' things nourish me:

More quotes for reflection:

In the ballroom of life, dance with resilience, for every misstep can be transformed into a graceful twirl towards success.

In life's dance, faith and fear take the lead. Faith dances with grace, while fear trips over its own steps. Pick one.

In the symphony of life, as your body aches with pain, let the strong spirit of your mind be your dance partner, guiding you through every graceful step of resilience.

In the midst of the dance of life, when the music falters and a loved one's melody fades, we find the strength to carry on, for their spirit becomes the guiding star in our dance of resilience.

In life's dance, we often weep behind a smiling mask.

In the grand ballroom of life, we often find ourselves performing a bittersweet waltz. It's a dance where we gracefully wear a mask of joy on the outside, even as tears quietly cascade within.

With each elegant step, we master the art of concealing our inner struggles, creating a facade of happiness that the world sees.

But beneath the glittering surface, our hearts may be heavy with sorrow. This dance is a poignant reminder of our strength, our ability to endure, and our capacity to show kindness even when our own souls ache.

In this intricate choreography of life, we learn that sometimes, the most beautiful performances are those where we smile on the outside while silently cradling our tears on the inside.

When she prayed for death, she found life's dance, where the darkest moments became the strongest beats in her rhythm of resilience.

In the intricate choreography of life, finding mental health is like the graceful waltz amidst the daily tasks—washing dishes, making beds, and pulling weeds. These simple pleasures compose the music that allows us to dance through existence with harmony and joy.

Life's dance reveals its beauty when I embrace every problem, for in them, I discover the strength God bestowed upon me, and I move through the steps of gratitude, knowing I can shoulder any tune with resilience.

When she had shed all the tears her heart could bear, she turned to the dance, and in its rhythmic embrace, her tears were replaced by the grace of resilience.

In her darkest hours, when all she desired was to fade away, life's dance compelled her to keep on living, and in that struggle, she found her strength.

Our words are powerful to ourselves. We tell our stories in many ways. Sometimes, we tell the same story differently to different people or for different reasons. How we tell the story can make us the victim or the hero. Do we seek sympathy, or do we look for the lesson? Our stories and the methods used to tell them can also help us discover our strengths and our resiliency.

However, even our strengths can be wrapped in a bit of scary, as told in this story.

The Dance of Resilience is a version captured initially for my grandkids.

Once upon a time in a small, weathered home nestled at the edge of the serene Kettle Moraine State Forest lived an elderly woman known to many as Grandma. Her life had been marked by the passing of loved ones, leaving her feeling as though she carried the weight of countless sorrows on her exhausted and dreary shoulders. Within two years, Grandma had endured the loss of her grandson by suicide, her beloved husband with a massive heart attack, her daughter from acute myeloid leukemia, her younger sister also by suicide, plus three more people who were a part of her family—leaving her with a heart heavy with grief. She couldn't understand why she was still alive.

For years, this grandma had found solace in cultivating her circle of friends and clients via her end-of-life coaching, hospice volunteering, and fostering communities of education, peace, strength, and inner solitude. Her retirement travels were more about renewal and retreats and less about venturing into the bustling world.

Even after several years of increasing solitude and emptiness, she maintained her inner strength and came to terms with what she termed the Covid hermitage life, rarely seeking her former social life. It was clear she was waiting to have her life over.

But as the years wore on and her empty life didn't seem to be over, she felt an unexplainable yearning deep within her soul, a longing for something she couldn't quite grasp. Her friends and some family had kindly suggested she should get a dog, find a new place to live, begin dating, or do something to fill the voids of life.

One summer day, as Grandma was alone in her home, she heard faint strains of music drifting through her open windows as a motorcyclist passed on the nearby road. Later that same day, she received a text message from her cousin, who lived many states away. This cousin had attached a short video clip of her dancing. Now Grandma's curiosity was piqued, for she knew her cousin was only one year younger than she herself. But the cousin looked so good, and her dancing was very good and so graceful.

This reminded Grandma of the package of dance lessons that Grandpa had purchased years earlier when she was planning to retire, and they were looking to add different activities into their lives. They had only used a couple of the lessons, as neither of them seemed much interested in the dancing aspects of reality. It wasn't for them.

Now life had changed, and being alone, thinking about the old package of dance lessons, she followed the melodious notes of these thoughts right back to thoughts of that original dance studio.

Summoning her courage, Grandma made a call, found that the lessons had never expired, and she could come take private dance lessons with a professional instructor. Wow! She was more impressed when she realized it had been fourteen years since the lessons were purchased and the studio had a new owner. And they STILL HONORED the lessons purchased! She knew this must be a gift from Richard, telling her it was time for things to change.

She drove to the studio where a group of dancers were busy practicing their graceful moves. The sight of their graceful movements stirred something within Grandma's heart, a longing she had long forgotten or maybe had never even possessed. Simultaneously, it stirred up thoughts of doubt, hesitation, and "I'm going right back home," though fortunately she was convinced, by a sweet woman named Lori, to just stay for that first lesson.

The dancers welcomed her with open arms, and she soon found herself learning the art of dance. It was a challenging journey, with her aging body often resisting the unfamiliar steps, but Gramma's determination was unwavering.

As weeks turned into months, Grandma's perseverance began to bear fruit. She learned to waltz, tango, and foxtrot with little bits of grace that belied her years. Each dance became a therapy session, a way for her to release the pent-up sorrow that had haunted her for so long.

Through dance, Grandma found not only physical strength but also emotional healing. She connected with others who had their own stories of loss and pain, and together they wove a tapestry of support and friendship. Grandma's heart, once weighed down by grief, now soared with the joy of each dance, each new friendship.

As Grandma continued to return to the dance floor, the music enveloped her. Sometimes it brought wonderful memories, and other times, the same music brought tears and tears and more tears. Yet, she continued and learned to dance with more grace and joy, and she began to share her new experiences. She found that her life changed and that the fact that she now found life filled with joy, which once seemed an impossibility, now brought inspiration to the hearts of others.

Grandma had discovered that, even in the midst of life's darkest storms, joy could be found again. Her journey from a place of deep sorrow to one of radiant happiness through the art of dance was an inspiration to all who knew her. The old woman had not only learned to dance but had learned to embrace life once more, proving that the human spirit could overcome even the heaviest of burdens.

I have told Hayk, the owner of that studio, many times that Richard was the one who brought me to the dance studio; however, it was he (Hayk) and Shem who kept me there. I continued to find people who I called my earth angels. Hayk was one of the first to appear. He remains a constant supporter of mine.

I am certain that in addition to dancing, it was the connections to wonderful people and the first small hesitant steps of establishing relationships that became my healing breath.

3.
Connection and Relationships

In my first year of dancing, I was so new to music and dance that it was easy to feel both pushed and pulled. One day I was at a lesson when Hayk, the studio owner, said, "Janet, I have your song."

What? I have a song? He said it was for my showcase or spotlight. I had no idea what any of that meant. He proceeded to tell me the song was titled "I Didn't Know My Own Strength." It was sung by Whitney Houston. I knew of her, and I admired her powerful voice. When I later looked up the lyrics, tears just flowed.

"I Didn't Know My Own Strength"
Whitney Houston

Ooh, yeah
Lost touch with my soul
I had nowhere to turn, I had nowhere to go
Lost sight of my dream
Thought it would be the end of me
I, I thought I'd never make it through
I had no hope to hold on to
I, I thought I would break
I didn't know my own strength
And I crashed down, and I tumbled
But I did not crumble
I got through all the pain
I didn't know my own strength

Survived my darkest hour, my faith kept me alive

I picked myself back up, hold my head up high

I was not built to break

I didn't know my own strength, oh

Found hope in my heart

I found the light to light my way out of the dark

Found all that I need

Here inside of me, oh

I thought I'd never find my way

I thought I'd never lift that weight

I thought I would break

I didn't know my own strength

And I crashed down, and I tumbled

But I did not crumble

I got through all the pain

I didn't know my own strength

Survived my darkest hour, my faith kept me alive

I picked myself back up, hold my head up high

I was not built to break

I didn't know my own strength

There were so many times I

Wondered how I'd get through the night, I

Thought I took all that I could take

I didn't know my own strength

And I crashed down, and I tumbled

But I did not crumble

I got through all the pain, oh

I didn't know my own strength
My faith kept me alive
I picked myself back up, I hold my head up high
I was not built to break
I didn't know my own strength, mmm-hm-hm
I was not built to break, no, no
I got to know my own strength

Songwriters: Diane Eve Warren.

There was NO WAY I could dance to that. None. I listened to the song until I heard the parts:

Lost touch with my soul
I had nowhere to turn,
I had nowhere to go

And I crashed down, and I tumbled
But I did not crumble
I got through all the pain

I fell apart inside and could not stop the tears. Those words went right through me and resonated with a ton of emotions. Fast forward, Hayk choreographed a beautiful dance, and with two amazing partners, I did manage to perform with them for my first dance fantasy number.

What no one knows (until now) is that I listened for the music to begin and also for the one part where the word crash was sung. I blocked out the other music and focused only on my steps.

And this was exactly where we needed to be when I heard the word crash.

Dance through life with others, for it's in our connections that the true beauty of the choreography emerges. In the waltz of existence, our deepest relationships provide the music.

In the dance of life, our deepest connections are the most exquisite moves, and the relationships we nurture are the heartbeats of our rhythm.

> Life's dance, a weave of hearts and grace,
> Connections formed in each embrace.
> From strangers to friends, bonds hold clear,

In life's waltz, we conquer fear.

Each step and turn, a treasure rare,
In love and friendship, joys we share.
So cherish the dance, each fleeting glance,
In life's ballet, we find our chance.

Connections and relationships can be compared to the interplay between a lighthouse and the ships navigating the vast waters.

The lighthouse stands as a beacon of hope, guidance, and security—much like the relationships we build with others. Its light reaches out across the dark waters, offering direction and comfort to ships in need, just as our meaningful connections can provide support and guidance both while on and off the dance floor as we navigate through life's challenges.

Our relationships thrive when we reach beyond ourselves, offering care, understanding, and trust to those around us. These connections serve as beams of light illuminating a different part of our journey, helping us navigate the uncertainties of life.

Ships turn and rely on the lighthouse just as we lean on our relationships for encouragement and strength. The interplay is mutual—ships depend upon the lighthouse to avoid danger, and the lighthouse fulfills its purpose through the presence of those guides. In this way, relationships are reciprocal. They are built on trust, communication, and the willingness to share both light and shadow.

A lighthouse may stand alone, on a rugged shore, but its true purpose is realized through its connection to the ships it guides. Likewise, we may feel isolated at times, but the bonds we form with others are what give our lives meaning and depth. For in these connections, we find both the strength to endure the storms, and the shared joy of a calm sea—knowing that we are never truly alone.

Clarifying Questions to Self:

What connections are most valuable to me?

What relationship do I most want to improve?

Why is this relationship important to me?

What's the smallest thing I can do right now to improve this relationship?

Are there new connections I want to make, and why?

More quotes for reflection:

In the dance of life, ask yourself: Are you a giver or a taker on this dance floor? Giving adds grace and joy, while taking casts shadows of selfishness.

Dance is not a solo act but a symphony of movement where we compete passionately, yet our true strength lies in lifting each other's spirits on this shared stage.

Dance through life, leaving footprints that make the world brighter, for a true dancer leaves a place better than they found it.

Knowing she would never find a partner on the dance floor who could fill her need for love, she danced with hope, for in the music's embrace, she found a love of her own, one that started within her heart.

Dance class can be a beautiful journey of self-discovery, even if you arrive seeking a partner but find yourself dancing solo, for it's in those solo steps that you often discover the rhythm of your own heart before intertwining it with another's.

On the dance floor of existence, two souls twirl and spin, birthing a new life in their elegant movements, a gift to us all who bear witness to the enchanting choreography of creation.

Our loving Creator gifted us with a beautiful sense of humor, and in embracing it, we honor the divine intention for joy and connection in our lives. To laugh and share laughter is to fulfill God's expectation for us, to express the love and light within us.

Life's paradox lies in the fact that through people, we may endure wounds, but it's also through people that we find the profound healing of understanding, forgiveness, and connection.

In life's intricate dance, love and pain often twirl hand in hand, leaving us to waltz between them, uncertain of the steps we're taking.

Life is a dance, and ballroom dancing is the graceful choreography that teaches us the beauty of partnership, the rhythm of connection, and the art of finding harmony in every step.

Dancing became the stepping stones, and yet there were constant questions I asked of myself.

Was it becoming my passion or an obsession? How would I determine the difference? There can be a fine line between the two.

Was it serving as a medication to just dull my reality? I continued to dance while realizing my healing journey was far from over. Self-awareness brought more questions.

One thing became clearer. It was the connections and the relationships that made me keep returning to the studio and the dance floor. I would continue to delve into clarifying my passion and understanding what was to become my purpose.

4.
Passion and Purpose

It's full of rewards and awards. The dancers are always being acknowledged for each step in their journey. Skilled coaches, with years of dancing, competing, teaching expertise, and personal experience, are available and relentless in providing students with valuable tips, encouragement, and direction for our improvement.

Everything with the Fred Astaire is about creating successes and noting every step of attainment on the path of joy. Find your passion, and life's dance will be a joyful celebration of purpose. Dance with purpose, and every step becomes a meaningful contribution to the world.

I say that, also knowing there are times I am on the dance floor with my partner, beginning a dance while thinking, "Which dance is this?" Maybe it's true that during some of our days, it's okay if we just wait until that purpose makes itself known. On these days, we just step on the dance floor and allow ourselves to be led. It's back to my theory of shut up and follow.

In the dance of life, passion is the music that moves us, and purpose is the choreography that gives our steps meaning.

Early on in life, I was 'given' my purpose. It was to get the chores done before you engaged in anything fun.

I grew up in a home where purpose was dictated: chores before fun, responsibility for my eight younger siblings. In my world, it was always about work. I grew up in a household where there was one voice, and it was not mine.

We were never asked what we thought nor what we felt. We were evaluated by what we had accomplished. My mother always introduced me as her right-hand girl. It was the way she saw me. It was the way she treated me. It was what she expected of me. Her identity of me shaped my view of myself as someone valued for what I accomplished rather than who I was. Fun wasn't a priority—it wasn't my world.

So today when others are having fun in the form of social games, I tend to withdraw. I do not know how to ride a bike, I do not know how to swim, I do not know how to play tennis, and the list goes on. That's just not my world, and even after all these years, fun still feels more terrifying than comfortable.

Dance became a mirror for life: sometimes the steps were clear, and other times, I simply had to trust my partner and follow. The studio fostered a space where successes were celebrated and even missteps had meaning. I found myself returning, not just for the movement, but for the connection.

Until a few years ago, I did not know how to dance. That is changing. But I do notice that if I am at a dance where it becomes more social and the dance steps are less clear, I tend to get very uncomfortable very quickly. These would be the times I have made an excuse and disappeared.

Someone called this silent leaving a French exit. Yes, I'm guilty. Alone I go… and I will be the first to admit being alone is not always lonely.

But sometimes it is.

I have found that I hate getting all dressed up to go out for a Friday night dance party—only to come home alone. I still have not gotten accustomed to that feeling. It leaves me wondering if I will ever find passion again. So far, it comes and goes as I wait for life to settle.

My purpose is to remain fluid now. As I stated earlier in this time of many changes, I am receptive to redirection. I know there is something more for me to do (or to be) in life. God and I are still having this conversation. He is obviously teaching me to find my patience.

Passion and purpose can be likened to a lighthouse standing resolute on the shore, its beam cutting through the night with unwavering intensity. The lighthouse's purpose is clear—to guide ships safely through turbulent waters.

It is driven by a singular mission: to be a source of light in the dark, ensuring that those at sea can find their way. Just as the lighthouse's light shines through fog and storm, passion is the inner fire that fuels our purpose, driving us to keep moving forward, even when the path is unclear.

When I watch my current dance partner Prezemyslaw and his wife Magdalena perform on the dance floor, I see this fire of passion burning brightly. It exemplifies their love of dance, of teaching, and of performing. Similar to other professional dancers, they are extremely dedicated, full of purpose, and passionate about what they do. This is contagious and inspiring.

The lighthouse does not question its role or value. It simply fulfills its purpose with determination and consistency. Similarly, when we are connected to our purpose, there is a sense of clarity, a deep knowing that what we do matters. Our passion is the fuel that powers that light, keeping it bright, even in moments of doubt or difficulty.

Passion gives our purpose life and energy, much like the flame that powers the lighthouse's beam. Without that inner drive, the light would fade, leaving the ships lost in the dark. But with passion, our purpose remains clear and strong, no matter how rough the seas around us become. The lighthouse doesn't change its mission based upon the weather; it shines whether the sea is calm or stormy.

Likewise, true purpose doesn't waver based upon external circumstances. When we are aligned with our passion, we continue to move towards our goals with perseverance and dedication.

> In life's grand dance, with each graceful twirl,
> Passion ignites, like a radiant pearl.
> It's the music that beckons, the fire within
> Guiding our steps through thick and thin
>
> So let passion light our heart's desire,
> And purpose be our steady guide.
> Together they'll lead us on,
> Into life's dance, clear and strong

In the end, the lighthouse stands as a symbol of the power of living with passion and purpose. It illuminates the way, not only for itself but also for others who may be lost.

In following our passion and staying true to our purpose, we not only create a fulfilling path for ourselves but also inspire and guide those around us. There is nothing sweeter than having a complete stranger come up to you and tell you how you've made a difference in their life.

Conversely, there is nothing sadder than wishing you could've made a difference for another as you must accept the consequences of their choices.

Earlier, I mentioned that the first of seven deaths within this two-year period was our twenty-four-year-old grandson's, and it was at his hand.

Two days after my daughter's death, I was at the funeral home assisting my granddaughter in making arrangements for her mother's services. I couldn't have imagined life being at a lower point.

I was wrong.

A few hours later, I arrived home and received a phone call from my youngest sister. Earlier I had shared a draft copy of my daughter's obituary and sent it to my sisters for a quick review to make sure I hadn't missed anyone or misspelled any names.

When she called me, I assumed it was in regard to the draft obituary. It was not. I was confused with her words until I finally understood that she was telling me another one of our sisters was dead.

By. Her. Own. Hand.

I couldn't comprehend, I couldn't breathe, and I didn't want to accept this information. This sister, who committed suicide, was one of the most engaged in her life, her church, and her church community. She homeschooled her children all the way through school; she was extremely patient, and everything I wasn't. And now she wasn't. Wasn't here. Wasn't going to ever be here. What in the hell was going on?

It would take many unanswered questions. Every feeling remaining from Jacob's suicide instantly flashed back and filled my mind. Why? Why? Why?

If I could become more numb, it happened here. There comes a point where thoughts and feelings totally stop.

Our purpose and our passions are not something we can redirect to another. In the end, we just accept the finality of their choices, their lives, and their outcomes. We don't have to like the choices; however, it helps to acknowledge everything in life falls into one of our two circles: control or concern. But that's a complete presentation on its own, and if you were ever in one of the Franklin Covey presentations I facilitated, you understand how we navigate between those two circles.

This death was nothing I could control. My daughter and my sister were both cremated on the same day. Across the country from each other, yet on the same day. One family, unimaginable grief, and not available to support each other. Similar to many things during the Covid nightmare, people were isolated, hurting, and unsure of the future and awaiting the time when passions and purposes could arise from these ashes of too many separated families and too many people hurting.

Maybe it's just a reminder that our passion and purpose are always on display. Even when there are no awards.

Especially when the failures are visible, there is still another step to be taken.

I continue to seek guidance and clarity as my journey moves forward. I have known from day one that I am not dancing for the medals, ribbons, or trophies. My reasons are different. I am dancing because for now, it keeps me alive. I hope my story inspires others to connect with their passions and to become clear about their purpose.

If I can find a way to blend book signing events, speaking engagements, and dance competitions into one travel date, there may be a way to dance even more.

Clarifying Questions to Self:

What am I most passionate about?

If you asked me what my main life purpose is, I would have to say it includes this:

What do I want, and why is this important to me?

More quotes for reflection:

In life's journey, setting an intention is like charting the course on a map; it guides your steps towards purpose and destination.

Dance through life, casting your contributions like seeds to the wind, for the beauty lies in not knowing where they'll bloom.

As the music fades and the final curtain falls, you'll wonder if your dance was enough. Remember, it was the authenticity of your steps that truly mattered.

In the dance of life, we often seek answers without knowing the question. As we move to the music of uncertainty, the steps we take may reveal the questions we never knew we had.

Midnight caller, where are you? In the realm of dreams, I search for answers in the shadows of night, seeking the whispers of the universe.

If compassion and hate were pills on life's shelf, I believe the pill of compassion would sell out first, for it's the dance of love that truly fills our hearts.

In the grand dance of life, just as we must leave the womb to begin our earthly journey, so too shall we one day step away from this existence, for in each transition, a new chapter of our cosmic journey begins.

When life laid her down, she arose with grace, wearing the robes of satisfaction and fulfillment as her dance of existence continued.

In life's intricate dance, our deepest desires are often not for the answers themselves but the yearning to find the right questions to ask, for therein lies the path to enlightenment and self-discovery.

In the rhythm of life's fiery dance, burning so hot and bright, one's light shines so intensely that even the darkness opens its arms to welcome the brilliant night.

As her body throbbed with passion, her soul whispered, 'Fly with me,' and together they wove a dance of boundless ecstasy.

In the grand tapestry of life's dance, the Almighty, the teacher of all, weaves the threads of wisdom and guidance, inspiring every step, every fall.

Dance to your own rhythm, and you find your joy in the spotlight; remember, while they're paid to teach and partner, you're paid in satisfaction and happiness.

Her body craves the rhythm of love, her mind hungers for its sweet embrace, yet her heart whispers, 'Not yet, for in patience, the dance becomes a masterpiece.

In her life's dance, she searched for love yet realized that sometimes, before finding someone to dance with, she needed to tend to the steps of daily life—mowing the grass, shoveling the snow, getting groceries, and cleaning the house—for love often meets us while we're tending to the rhythms of our own existence.

In the dance of life, her steps create a masterpiece, and the smile she wears is the canvas of her soul, painted with the colors of success.

When your fiery dance dims, and all that's left are ashes, remember that even in embers, the potential for a new spark remains.

This next part may seem redundant, yet it shows how to incorporate some of the principles using my experience and knowledge of both Appreciative Inquiry and the universal Laws of Attraction. The best part of these shows how the questions we ask and the things we tell ourselves are instrumental in the answers we receive. This is a key learning in life.

Our life is our story. We tell it in our thoughts, in our beliefs, with our words, and ultimately, by our actions. We retell it until it makes sense, until the lessons come forth, and until it forms our future direction and action. And then we create new meanings from our old stories.

So, from a different view, this retells the same story, showing how life is interconnected and ever so simple in its reach to engage others.

Sometimes, we tell the same story from a different location. I was extremely fortunate to attend a competition in Hawaii. It was the Star Ball. There was so much beauty and so many beautiful people. There were families enjoying time together as we inculcated dance with destiny. It was fun.

It was fun even as I carried the rock of darkness into the light and beauty. How does one forget when the emptiness keeps filling every possible moment? With my years in my challenging career, I am good at covering those emotions.

Richard was one who could always tell when things weren't good with me. He said, "It shows in your eyes." He wasn't in Hawaii, and I did my best to show up and enjoy my amazing people.

5.
Incorporating Law of Attraction Principles to Dance

Once upon a time, while in a dance competition in a picturesque hotel in Honolulu, Grandma decided to capture a piece of her story. For this writing, she will refer to herself as Grandma.

She was known by many in her community as the wise "Law of Attraction Coach," a title she had earned after her retirement by learning and eventually mentoring students for the international life coach Christy Whitman. In addition to becoming a hospice volunteer after retiring, Grandma found joy through the recent decade of helping people manifest their dreams and desires.

But Grandma's journey of being a Law of Attraction coach was anything but ordinary. Because of her profound experiences with hospice, she had created her niche of interviewing many people facing death. As her coaching world expanded, she became known as an end-of-life coach, helping those who were approaching an impending death of a loved one.

Many of her thoughts and experiences were shared in her first published book, *I'm Sorry, I Love You, Goodbye: Harvesting the sacred gifts of the final days.*

None of this initially seemed helpful when she had faced her own unimaginable tragedy as she lost those seven beloved people in her life—her grandson, husband, daughter, sister, sister-in-law, and two very dear friends—all within a short span of time, and six of these deaths occurred during the Covid pandemic, meaning she wasn't able to be with them during a most critical time. It was a storm of grief that could have easily drowned her spirit. And for a couple of years, it did exactly that as she struggled with the question of why she was still alive when much of her reason for living had disappeared.

In the midst of her suffering, Grandma found solace in dance. It was her late husband Richard who, without them knowing it at the time—introduced her to the world of dance when he purchased a package of social dance lessons years prior when she had retired from her postal executive job.

Dance now became a way to cope with the pain. At first, Grandma was hesitant, but as she moved to the rhythm of the music, something magical happened. She felt a profound connection between her movements and the universe around her. It was as if the dance was a bridge between her sorrowful heart and the cosmos itself.

One evening, while practicing her dance moves, Grandma had a vision. She realized that the Law of Attraction principles she had been teaching to others could be applied to her own life and her newfound passion for dance. She decided that if she could attract happiness and abundance through the power of her thoughts, she could also use it to heal her heart and become the dancer in a way she had never dreamed possible.

Grandma began her journey by visualizing herself as a graceful and confident dancer, with the wind caressing her hair and the waves of the water echoing her movements. Okay, that may be exaggerated; however, it was her story to create. She diligently applied many of the Law of Attraction principles—including focusing on her goals, maintaining a positive attitude, and expressing gratitude for every small improvement in her dancing.

As the months passed, Grandma's inner transformation was a bit miraculous. Her once-aching heart grew lighter, and her dance became a mesmerizing spectacle for others who saw her. (Work with me here, as it's still her 'created' story.) She had not only made great strides in healing her own pain but had also inspired others with her story of resilience and transformation.

One summer day, a local writer, Nancy, who had been witnessing Grandma's performance, decided it was a story worth telling. Impressed by her passion, dedication, and the sheer joy she brought to the art of dance, Nancy offered to write an article for the local newspaper. It was an honor for Grandma to share a part of her story about how she had manifested her desires through the power of the Law of Attraction.

Grandma's journey didn't end there. She continued to inspire and coach others, not only in manifesting their desires but also in using their passions as a means of healing and self-discovery. Her story serves as a testament to the incredible potential of the human spirit to rise above even the darkest of times.

And so, Grandma continues to dance through life, teaching others the beauty of turning their dreams into reality, all while healing her own heart one graceful step at a time.

Our language is powerful, and the words we tell others and, more importantly, the words we tell ourselves tend to play out in our reality. Richard used the term "mind over matter" to describe this.

I have a more recent example. In early December of last year, I arrived home following a total knee replacement. I was hoping all would go well, but I did not control the surgical part of it. For that, I depended upon the doctor to do his job. He did.

I drove the four hours to the clinic, had the surgery, and recovered in a local hotel for a few days before driving home without incident. I knew that if I needed to, I could stop after each hour and would eventually be home within a few days. It was not as though I didn't have family to drive me home. I hadn't asked them. And when my granddaughter in Minnesota came to visit me as I recovered following the surgery, she was quite insistent that she drive me home. Not wanting to impose on any of my family, I was equally insistent that I was fine (how many times do we say I am fine, I can handle this when people are sincerely offering their help?).

Prior to the surgery, I knew that the outcome was not guaranteed. I agreed to a new dance fantasy choreography. I agreed, unsure of my ability to perform the new dance within a few months. The one thing that was certain was my determination to do my part.

Before the surgery, I stopped at the physical therapist's office and requested a printout of the exercises that I would need to do post-surgery. My thought was it would be easier to learn to do the exercises before I was in pain.

I did the exercises, rested, and managed my thoughts.

Instead of using the language of hurting, I chose the language of healing. So, whenever someone would ask me if the knee was hurting, a likely response from me would be, "It's really healing today."

Ultimately, I was more than pleased to be able to dance our Dance Fantasy number with my partners, Przemyslaw and Arsen, at the end of March. Was it perfect? No, but most dances are not intended to be perfect.

I was very pleased with the outcome, and I think my dance partners would say the same. We did it! Within four months of a total knee replacement. Does it still hurt? Yes, it's still healing. I continue to heal, to learn, and to seek more balance and harmony in my life and on the dance floor.

Life is meant to be enjoyed. There are times when it becomes necessary to create fun. This is true even when nothing is going right. Take the time to find the balance.

I am now learning to relax and allow the fun to be more present. My instructor is a master at filling the learning with fun.

Fred Astaire creates the fun. It's the people at every level who insist that learning and enjoying are inseparable.

6.
Balance and Harmony

Balancing the various aspects of life is like mastering a perfect dance routine. Seek harmony in your life's dance, for it's in the balance that you find true serenity.

In the dance of life, balance and harmony are the graceful steps that lead us to the music of our soul.

In life's dance, we spin and sway,
Seeking balance day by day.
Through highs and lows, our spirits glow,
In harmony's gentle, endless flow.

With grace, we step, in chance, in trance,
Embracing each beat of life's grand dance.

How many times does an instructor ask his student, "Where are you?" This question is asked in regard to our balance: are we shifted forward, backward, to one side, or centered? When our partner knows where we are, they can then guide us forward into our next step.

Balance and harmony in life can be symbolized by our lighthouse, poised between the forces of land and sea, calm and storm, light and darkness.

The lighthouse stands as a mediator between these opposing forces, harmonizing the chaos of the ocean with the stability of the shore.

The lighthouse harmonizes the ocean's chaos with the shore's stability, embodying life's delicate balance. In the same way, balance is about finding that center point between various demands, emotions, and responsibilities we face in life, while harmony emerges when these elements coexist peacefully.

I acknowledged my impatience with both the advantages and disadvantages:

One of the advantages is having the ability to get things done quickly.

One of the disadvantages is losing interest after I've accomplished something.

Yes, I'm the fan in the seventh inning who makes an assessment of how the game is going and is ready to leave.

So, the challenge to myself now is to temper that impatience as I continue to learn dances.

I love learning new dances.

I cannot say the same for the competitions.

After spending decades of my career traveling and dealing with airports and hotels and being away from home, it's not high on my list to continue doing those things.

And yet I like to dance.

And I want to continually improve my dancing.

I love watching my dance partner and fellow students in competitions.

And at the same time, I breathe satisfaction into the fact that I'm not having hair and makeup session packing a half dozen dance dresses and sleeping in a hotel room.

Yes, I like dancing.

And I want to keep dancing.

I will find my balance.

I believe life will always offer us at least three options in every situation. Our job will be to pick one. Many of my dance photographers will catch this sign of inspiration. Others will hear me say, "Pick one."

The lighthouse does not resist the waves nor ignore the stillness of the sea. It exists in both states, rooted and strong, yet flexible enough to understand whatever comes.

Similarly, balanced means accepting both the highs and lows of life, knowing that both are necessary and natural. It's the ability to remain grounded in times of turbulence, just as the lighthouse remains firmly anchored, unshaken by the surging waters.

One element of dancing is learning to turn quickly without losing balance or becoming dizzy. I still struggle with this. As my dancing granddaughter Piper tells me, I need to learn the technique of spotting—focusing on one spot in the distance while allowing my body to turn.

The light from the lighthouse doesn't shine in all directions at once, nor does it fixate on one spot forever. It moves in a steady rhythmic circle, sweeping the sea and land with even attention. This represents harmony, the graceful and deliberate distribution of focus across different areas of life. Just as a lighthouse's light illuminates each part of the horizon in its time, harmony is found when we give the right amount of energy to different aspects of our lives, our family, dance, work, relationships, health, and personal growth.

In the stillness of the night or the fury of a storm, the lighthouse remains a symbol of stability and peace. It balances the contrasting elements around it, creating a sense of order.

Clarifying Questions to Self:

Where do I find my balance and harmony?

When my life is in balance, what does that look like, feel like, and sound like?

What is one small thing that I control and can change to bring more balance and harmony into my life?

More quotes for reflection:

In the dance of life, trust is the graceful step that leads to harmonious relationships and the rhythm of positive outcomes.

In the dance of life, remember to bow with gratitude to those who teach you the steps, for they light your path with wisdom and grace.

In the grand dance of life, imagine if every step were a joyful dance move, and every moment a celebration of fun.

In the dance of life, the mind takes the lead, its rhythm a frenetic pace, a frantic need. But sometimes, it yearns for a different sound, a melody soft, a quieter rebound. So the body, like a partner in a trance, slows its steps and begins a graceful dance. The mind and body, in harmonious sway, find balance together in their own special way. As the tempo slows, they both unwind, a moment of peace in the chaos of the mind. In this life dance, a lesson we have found is that sometimes, the mind needs to slow the body down.

In life's dance, a skilled partner transforms competition into a harmonious cooperation, gently quelling the anxiety that once plagued our steps.

Life's dance teeters on the delicate edge where our passion for a hobby meets the brink of obsession, much like the thin line that separates genius from insanity.

Like a river, life flows with both currents of exhaustion and those demanding we do more. Knowing when to swim against that tide of weariness and when to embrace the calm shores of rest and rejuvenation is extremely important—though sometimes difficult to decipher.

In the grand ballet of life, some may dance through a lifetime before realizing that the true gift lies not in the packaging but in the precious content it holds.

In the symphony of life, all prescriptions should be written in the language of dance, the serenity of swimming, the adventure of hiking, and the purpose of housework and yardwork, for therein lies the remedy for both body and soul.

Dance is where the rhythm of grace meets the elegance of prayer, a sacred symphony of movement that transcends the ordinary and touches the divine."

In the quiet company of a single coffee cup, I embrace the loneliness of dawn, for it's in these moments of solitude that I find strength to face the day ahead.

In life's dance, there are moments when we find ourselves not wanting to love and yet lacking the energy to hate. It's in these steps of indifference that we discover the power of inner strength and fortitude.

After finishing the first Vegas competition, where I had great results, receiving two scholarships and two championships in my category, I confessed to my dance partner, "I don't think I like dancing."

He gave me a strange look and was likely thinking, *What the hell's wrong with you?* But he didn't say it. He would never say that. Instead, he later sent me a text explaining how heartbreaking it was seeing me not happy because he saw it totally differently. He indicated that after the party, people had come up to him inquiring about me and offering amazing words.

What is next? He said we will sum up and discuss our accomplishments and together analyze everything. He stated that he and Hayk had watched me since the beginning and were proud.

"I think you don't even realize how great you did and how you amazed everybody, including your own instructor, with your spirit and attitude." He was correct. This was new to me as it was my first world championship. He said many people would love to come back home with 2 envelopes and being placed so well in our first World.

Given more reflection, I remembered my celebration drink at dinner. For me, alcohol of any kind serves as a depressant. It always has. Along with having success and not having Richard to share it, I was already in a funky mood. That was when I shared my reservations. Again, he put things into perspective.

Since then, I've realized there's not a certain dance nor a certain type of dance that I really love. I like them all. I like Smooth and Rhythm. I like anything that has me on the dance floor having fun.

What I figured out is that I love the mental challenge of learning something new.

So, the dance that I'm learning right now is my favorite.

And I think that will always be the case.

There will lie the challenge for my instructor. Just keep pushing me. In doing so, my job will be to trust and to follow, knowing that my instructor is the connection used by my Higher Power to communicate to me as I continue to find my purpose in life.

A fellow dance student described a term called fear of missing out (FOMO). I don't have that. My career required decades of travel with airports, hotels, and food that was anything but homemade. I like being home, and I like sleeping in my own bed. Balance, balance, balance.

"SHUT UP AND FOLLOW: EMBRACING THE DIVINE MESSAGE"

This is based upon a motto that a dance instructor would never say but was interpreted when one said the words "I will lead," and subsequently the student (Grandma) inculcated these words to mean shut up and follow. She later realized that this message may likely be coming to her from a much higher source. Though she laughingly will say shut up and follow to herself while on the dance floor, she knows there's much more to it, and the message was profound. She thanks Victor and Shem for allowing this message to resonate at this deeper and much higher level.

In the tapestry of life, there are moments when we find ourselves at crossroads, grappling with uncertainty, doubt, and confusion. During these trying times, it's not uncommon for people to search for guidance, a higher purpose, or a profound message that can illuminate their path. In such moments, it's fascinating to consider the idea that the divine message might be as simple as "shut up and follow."

Many spiritual and religious traditions teach us to surrender to a higher power, to have faith in a grander plan, and to trust that there's a purpose behind the events in our lives. This is often a challenging concept for many individuals who are used to being in control, making decisions, and forging their own destinies. However, the message of "shut up and follow" is not about relinquishing our autonomy or intelligence; instead, it's about embracing trust and acceptance in the face of uncertainty.

God, the universe, or whatever higher power one believes in often conveys this message through the circumstances and people in our lives. It's a gentle reminder that we don't always need to have all the answers, nor do we need to exert relentless control over our lives. Sometimes, it's about acknowledging that there is a greater plan at play, and our role is to listen and follow that divine guidance.

"I've got you; you must trust me."

These words, whispered by the cosmos itself, hold a profound truth. We are not alone on this journey through life. We are supported by an unseen force, and it's in our best interest to have faith in it. Trust is the foundation of this message. It's about having faith that the universe has our backs, that there is a purpose to our existence, and that we are being guided towards something greater than we can imagine.

"I know where we're going. I know where you're going, and I know how to get you there."

This part of the message reassures us that there is a destination, a purpose, and a path. It's an invitation to let go of the anxiety about the future and the regrets of the past.

Today is where we need to focus. The present moment is the only moment we have control over, and it's where we can make a difference in our lives. As her instructor, Przemyslaw says to take only the next step in climbing a mountain. Only one step. This step. It again implies a trust that we do not need to see the whole journey—just this next step. And then to trust that if we follow—step by step—the journey will unfold.

"I choose to dance in total appreciation, accepting God's message of shut up and follow."

This line reflects the profound shift in perspective that occurs when we embrace this divine message. It's about celebrating life, even in its uncertainty and imperfection. To "dance in total appreciation" is to find joy and gratitude in every moment, recognizing that every step, even the challenging ones, is a part of our unique journey.

In essence, the message "shut up and follow" is an invitation to let go of the need to control everything, to trust in the grand design of the universe, and to find contentment in the present moment. It's about acknowledging that there's a plan, even if we can't see it, and that we are not alone on this journey.

So, as you navigate the twists and turns of life, remember these words: "Shut up and follow." Embrace the guidance, trust, have faith in the journey, and dance in appreciation. In doing so, you might just find the profound wisdom and guidance you seek from the universe itself.

CONTENT ADVISORY

The following page contains discussions and imagery related to suicidal thoughts, firearms, and personal struggles. While these descriptions and images are included as part of my journey and decision to live, I recognize that such content may be distressing for some readers.

If you feel uncomfortable, you may choose to **skip this section** and continue reading at page 83.

Your well-being is important—please take care of yourself while reading.

Early in this publication, the book critics said I should include personal stories to make it real for you, the readers. The following is as personal as it will ever be.

I began this book mentioning some of the dark thoughts. I think they require a mention here for anyone who needs to hear it. Life holds dark places that are most willing to swallow us whole when we are at our lowest and most vulnerable points.

In the single month of January 2022, there were eight red S's marking different days on my calendar. On each of those dates, I seriously wanted my life over and found those were the times it was necessary to talk myself out of suicide. I didn't seek help because I did not want help. I did not want intervention. I just wanted it over.

Dancing changed this!

Since finding Fred Astaire and all of the wonderful people associated with it, I have had only one such night since. I vividly recall that at 11:34 p.m. on January 4, 2023, I couldn't sleep wrestling with my dark thoughts. I told myself it was decision time, and I made up my mind to finally stop the thoughts—get up and do it or swear to permanently stop wrestling with the choice.

A few minutes later, my kitchen counter held two guns with their associated ammunition. I opened my Google to research which had more force and thus would do the least amount of damage. I didn't want that. This needed to be permanent. The one with less force would take longer and do more internal damage.

Without sharing more information, I now knew what choice would work best for me. Given the choice and knowing it would be a choice with many consequences, I chose life.

Knowing the suffering for remaining family, I chose life—and put away the things on my counter. I kept the photos as a reminder that I have made a permanent choice and a commitment. I will honor this commitment.

Mental illness is real and if you do not want intervention, there's no way anyone, no matter how close, would possibly know or be able to stop it.

In addition to my family, who didn't deserve more pain and suffering, I must give much credit to Hayk and Shem for giving me a reason to choose life. From the bottom of my heart, thank you both. You both have heard me say that the awards mean nothing to me. I have nothing to prove and no one to prove it to. I dance because, for now, it's a very big part of what keeps me alive. You've made a difference in my life!

For anyone needing to talk, reach out to someone even if that someone is a complete stranger who will just listen. Though at the time, I couldn't see how, life CAN be good again. Life with dancing involved can be even better!

Conclusion

Dance therapy is a powerful tool for physical, emotional, and mental well-being, particularly for older adults facing grief, isolation, and health challenges. The author is advocating that dance should be recognized as a vital therapeutic practice.

The author's journey—from deep grief and isolation to rediscovering joy—demonstrates how dance therapy provides more than just movement; it restores purpose and connection.

Dance allows individuals to process grief and trauma in a natural, restorative way.

This author's testimony underscores that dance is not just an activity but is a critical medical option.

As older adults face increasing physical and emotional challenges, dance therapy provides improved balance, stability, and flexibility, reducing hospitalization risks. Learning dance patterns helps memory and may slow cognitive decline. Dance alleviates loneliness and depression by fostering structured social engagement.

Dance therapy is an essential tool for aging well, as it is medicine for the body, mind, and soul. Many community centers incorporate exercise and dance for older adults. It is now time to acknowledge and recognize dance as a legitimate therapy supported by doctors and healthcare providers.

Together, we've learned that dance is more than just steps and movements; it's a language of the heart. It's a testament to the power of unity, shared dreams, and the pure joy of moving to music.

So, to everyone who has been a part of this incredible journey, I want to say thank you. Thank you for making the dance floor a place where dreams come alive, where friendships flourish, and where we become the best versions of ourselves. Here's to the owners, coaches, instructors, and fellow students, and to the countless more memories and dances that await us on this extraordinary journey.

I know that this book is no longer without end; however, it is becoming the beginning of something more powerful, new, and exciting.

I now close with this dedication to my recent life partner and forever friend and with my thanks to those of you who've made a difference.

Richard,

Five years have passed since that somber day when we bid you our final farewells and returned your body to Mother Earth. With hearts scarred by the emptiness of your absence, your spirit remains ever present, holding our beautiful shared moments.

As I remain here today, your love continues to inspire me. Your strength, kindness, and unwavering support have left an indelible mark on my soul. I carry your love with me, and it gives me the strength to face these days.

I continue to honor your memory by living a life filled with the same love and compassion that you always showed to me. Thank you for dragging me out onto the dance floor. Know that I dance for you.

To my family,

You being in my life is incredibly beautiful. I love you, and love how much you support me in my journey and keep the fire in my heart.

I love watching you raise your families. I quickly acknowledge you are much better at parenting than I ever was. Thank you. I have hope in this world when I see the goodness, strength, and love in the coming generations.

I also want to express my heartfelt gratitude to the owners, coaches, instructors, and my fellow students who have made the dance floor a place of inspiration, growth, and sheer joy.

To the owners, thank you for providing us with this beautiful space where we can dance our hearts out, a sanctuary for self-expression, and a canvas for our dreams. Your dedication and commitment to the art of dance have created space for all of us.

To the coaches and instructors, you've been our guiding lights, mentors, and sources of wisdom. Your patience, expertise, and unwavering support have shaped us into the dancers we are today. Your passion for teaching has ignited our passion for dancing.

To my fellow students, you are more than just dance partners; you are friends, comrades, and fellow dreamers. We've shared more than a few hours of practice, celebrated each other's victories, and lifted one another during moments of doubt. The dance floor has been a place where we've grown not only as dancers but also as a dancing community.

CREATE THE MOMENTS THAT MATTER WHILE YOU STILL CAN.

This motto was the core of my End-of-Life coaching work. It held much value then and even more today. We are not promised tomorrow.

In the meantime, "Let's dance!"

About the Author

Dr. Janet Bieschke, with over thirty years of experience as an Operations Manager, holds a Doctorate in Organization Change from Pepperdine University and an Executive MBA from the University of Wisconsin-Milwaukee. She is also a certified End-of-Life Coach, dedicated to providing compassionate guidance during life's most significant transitions.

At 70, Janet embraced a new chapter by studying ballroom dance, demonstrating her commitment to lifelong learning and the joy of discovering new passions. Her expertise, empathy, and adventurous spirit continue to inspire others to pursue excellence and embrace change at any stage of life.

However, her most cherished and fulfilling roles will always be as a mother, grandmother, and now, a proud great-grandmother.

Contact Information
Janet.bieschke@icloud.com
920-946-8413

www.ingramcontent.com/pod-product-compliance
Lightning Source LLC
Chambersburg PA
CBHW041252290625
28745CB00001B/1